Also by Janine Kovac

SPINNING: Choreography for Coming Home

Anthologies

Mamas Write: 29 Tales of Truth, Wit, and Grit

Tiny Feet, Giant Steps: Portraits of Miracles in the Alta Bates Summit Newborn Intensive Care Unit

Multiples Illuminated: A Collection of Stories and Advice from Parents of Twins, Triplets and More

Nothing But the Truth So Help Me God:51 Women Reveal the Power of Positive Female Connection

Praise for BRAIN CHANGER

"The science of mind—cognitive science—is anything but dry and abstruse. It is about how to live. Up to 98% of thought is unconscious, and the science takes you into the ideas you live by but don't know you have. Janine Kovac figured this out under the most extreme stress: becoming the mother of premature twins not given much chance to survive, while finishing her cognitive science degree and raising a two-year-old. *Brain Changer* is an inspiring, hard-to-put-down book of how she used her cognitive science to bring her one-and-a-half pound twins and herself through a mother's nightmare to healthy happy lives."

—George Lakoff, UC Berkeley, *New York Times* bestselling author of *Don't Think of an Elephant*

"Most people don't know that they need to have a little cognitive science under their belts in order to parent well, but read this book and you'll know that probably, you do. It's a useful and interesting tool for much more skillful—and therefore effective and joyful—parenting."

—Christine Carter, Ph.D., author of *Raising Happiness* and *The Sweet Spot*

"*Brain Changer* is a perfect gem of a book. Kovac weaves together cognitive science, language and metaphor, and deeply moving personal stories of difficult moments at the beginning and end of life. With candor, humor, and authenticity, *Brain Changer* offers a way through trying times not just for parents, but for everyone. I highly recommend this engaging and helpful book."

—Lorrie Goldin, Licensed Clinical Social Worker

"Any parent who has experienced loss will soak up the wisdom of this book. Janine Kovac has a unique talent for taking raw experiences and bringing them to life with deep insight, candor and a unique perspective. Her background in dance, cognitive science and directing all come together in a production that is dazzling."

—Maria Ramos-Chertok, Rockwood Leadership Institute and author of *The Butterfly Series Workbook and Journal*

"*Brain Changer* offers a fascinating look at how Janine Kovac used language to reframe her world during a time of extreme trauma. This book is a good read with lessons easily applied to everyday life for all of us."

—Marianne Lonsdale, co-founder, Write on Mamas

Brain
CHANGER

A mother's guide to cognitive science

Brain
CHANGER

A mother's guide to cognitive science

JANINE KOVAC

Brain Changer: A Mother's Guide to Cognitive Science

Copyright © 2016 by Janine Kovac

All rights reserved. No part of this publication may be reproduced, stored in or introduced into a retrieval system, or transmitted, in any form, or by any means electronic, mechanical, printing, recording or otherwise, without the prior permission of the author and/or publisher.

Author Photo by Terry Lorant

Cover Design and Interior Typesetting by Melissa Williams Design

Front image ©2019 by Feodora, Adobe Stock

SECOND EDITION ISBN: 978-0692782224

Published by Noelle & Noelle

for Mom and Dad
who are always game to discuss a metaphor

INTRODUCTION

After completing my degree in cognitive science at UC Berkeley, I became pregnant with what my husband and I thought was our second child. Then, surprise! We were having twins. I had never given much thought to how a twin pregnancy could be different from what I'd already experienced. Then, halfway through our first ultrasound, the sonographer excused herself and returned a few minutes later with the doctor to verify her findings. Usually babies (twins or not) develop in their own gestational sacs. However in my case, my boys were sharing both a placenta and an amniotic sac. It was a 1-in-45,000 kind of pregnancy.

Sharing the same space meant there was nothing to keep the umbilical cords from tangling, braiding, and knotting together. And if one twin died in utero, there would be no way to save the healthy twin—we would lose them both. A crimped cord that cuts circulation to the point of asphyxiation was not inevitable, but it was unpredictable and unpreventable. The odds of survival without complications hovered at about 50%.

After carefully outlining the risks and the protocols our doctor said to me, "There is nothing you can do to prevent the babies from dying. Don't let it stress you out. You can't do anything about it."

And then he sent me home.

There was anger. There was denial. There was panic. And there was lots of Googling.

But there was something else, too. A thesis I'd just written titled "A Cognitive Linguistic Analysis of Parenting." As the parent of a toddler girl, I was trying to make sense of the parenting books I'd read. Should I sleep train or not? How early should I teach her to read? And: if all these people were experts, why didn't they all agree?

I took a novel approach to answering my questions. I analyzed the metaphors that parenting experts used to describe morality, emotional development, and human nature. This analysis became the topic of my thesis, which was awarded the Robert J. Glushko Prize for Distinguished Undergraduate Research in Cognitive Science. In the brief time between graduating from college and discovering that I was pregnant, I entertained fantasies of turning that thesis into a book.

Talking to doctors about my risky pregnancy turned out to be a lot like reading conflicting opinions from parenting experts. One doctor thought I should be on 24/7 bed rest. Another saw no problem with light exercise. One doctor advised, "Try not to think about it." Another reminded me, "You have to be prepared at every ultrasound to have a dead baby."

An undergraduate in cognitive science learns the basics of neural networks: when some neurons are activated, other networks must be inhibited. It's called mutual inhibition. It's the reason you can't feel fear and joy at the same time. Fear activates your fight-or-flight resources while joy makes you want to stop and smell the roses. Cognitive science students, at least the ones at UC Berkeley, learn something else, too. They learn that words and concepts are directly connected to neural networks. In other words, fear-related thought and messaging is directly connected to a network. Joy-related messaging is directly connected to a different network. If you could activate the joy-network through words, then you'd simultaneously inhibit the fear-network. The doctor's advice, "Try not to think about it" was actually not that ridiculous. And according to my thesis, I already knew how to do it.

My research had brought other resources into my orbit. Most notably, the Greater Good Science Center, a research center partially funded by UC Berkeley that focused on positive psychology. Christine Carter was the executive director at the time. Her writing and research were extremely beneficial. Her choice of words regarding nurturance, altruism, social connections, and gratitude helped me build the geeky computational models that I needed for my academic paper. What's more—these same models became the tools I needed to build a "happiness" road map for all stressful situations that were about to come my way.

Which was a great thing, since my high-risk pregnancy was just the beginning of my challenges as the mother of twins. I went into labor before I hit the six-month mark and my babies were born via emergency Cesarean section.

One twin was born weighing a pound and a half. The other weighed a pound and twelve ounces. They were a foot long.

The boys spent the next three months in the newborn intensive care unit (NICU) where they had IVs, breathing tubes, feeding tubes, x-rays, blood transfusions, and surgery to fix their heart murmurs.

I clung to the ideas and abstract concepts of my thesis, hoping that these ideas would keep fear and panic at bay. I also tried making lots of jokes. (Note: nurses don't really appreciate the jokes as mu ch as you think they will.)

It worked—sort of. Having a newborn in the hospital is devastating. Our boys weren't expected to live. And if they did live, they were expected to be disabled or have extreme cognitive deficits. Cognitive science was my crutch. Crutches don't heal a broken foot; they just help you get around. After the boys left the hospital, ostensibly healthy but with another two years of early intervention therapy ahead of them, Christine Carter asked me to share some of my cognitive science techniques on her website. Originally my posts were supplemental testimonials to her book *Raising Happiness: 10 Simple Steps for More Joyful Kids and Happier Parents.* Each blog post directly related to one of the steps in her book, but it also introduced an aspect of cognitive science from my thesis, a concept that helped me bridge the gap between what I read from the Greater Good Center and how I actually applied it to my life.

In this book, I've included several of the blog posts from that series as well as a little scientific back story. The essays explore some of the techniques that helped me cope as a mom: the practical application of putting on my oxygen mask, expressing gratitude, managing flow, and cultivating a growth mindset—but with a twist of cutting-edge cognitive science.

1
All Bad News is My Bad News: The Salient Exemplar Effect

In August 2009 I discovered that I was pregnant with twins—a rare, 1-in-45,000 kind of pregnancy in which the twins shared both a placenta and an amniotic sac. The protocol for this kind of pregnancy is to monitor the mother and babies twice a month. If the mother is still pregnant at 28 weeks, she is admitted into the hospital until the babies are born.

A normal pregnancy is 40 weeks, but for a mono-amniotic/mono-chorionic pregnancy such as mine, the best-case scenario is that the babies are delivered around 32 weeks' gestation—the point at which the risk of the twins dying from prematurity is less than the risk of dying from umbilical cord entanglement in the womb. Babies born 8 weeks early may still need help to breathe and eat. Although many do quite well, they are still at risk for learning and behavioral problems later in their development.

You don't have to be a cognitive scientist to know that in the face of scary and uncertain circumstances humans often act irrationally. I knew I was asking for trouble by Googling search terms such as "mortality rates for preemies." But I did it anyway. I learned about horrendous fetal birth defects that I never knew existed and found entire forums of scared mothers.

The truth of the matter was that I had stumbled upon tragic circumstances that were actually quite rare and none of them had anything to do with mono-amniotic pregnancies. But the more I read about these worst-case scenarios, the more probable it seemed that they would happen to me.

Cognitive scientists call this the **salient exemplar effect**—a memorable or tragic event makes such a great impact we assume that it happens more frequently than it actually does. For example, (statistically speaking) terrorist attacks and plane crashes are quite rare when compared to other accidents or acts of violence. And the likelihood that a terrorist attack will cause a plane crash is even less likely. Yet the tragic events of 9/11 frightened many people into thinking that air travel was riskier than it actually is.

For the first few months of my pregnancy, I scoured the web for information about preemies, trying to guess what would happen if our babies were born 5 weeks before their due date—or 8 weeks or 10 weeks. Sometimes I'd try to distract myself with my regular "mom duties," such as taking care of my then-two-year-old daughter. But as soon as I'd tuck her into bed, I'd sneak back to my computer to ask questions of preemie moms on parenting forums and look at images of very tiny wrinkled babies hooked up to tubes and sensors in plastic boxes.

The more I researched, the more pessimistic I grew regarding our chances of having healthy, normal babies. I knew that my illogical conclusions were the result of salient exemplars but Internet research made me feel informed. Regardless of how irrational it was, I was afraid that if I didn't read about worst-case scenarios then I wouldn't be prepared for one.

However, the Internet also has the power to connect us. I reached out to everyone I knew who had twins: friends, friends of friends, colleagues of friends. One of my friends emailed me back recommending a book specifically for pregnant mothers of twins. The author was a doctor who specialized in twin pregnancies and maternal-fetal nutrition. (The book, by Dr. Barbara Luke, was *When You're Expecting Twins, Triplets, or Quads.*)

There were tips for healthy light exercise, tips for resting throughout the day (and night), tips for talking to your employer about maternity leave, and, of course, tips for eating. In fact, one-third of the book was recipes for nutritious meals for pregnant moms.

My friend ended her email with this question: "Janine, can you eat 4000 calories a day?"

She explained: "If you can gain twenty pounds in the first half of the pregnancy, you'll increase your chances of having healthy-weight babies."

There was so much that was beyond my control, but I could do this: I could eat big healthy meals. I could rest when I was tired and I could spend time with my husband and my young daughter. My new plan of action didn't make my anxiety go away completely. It didn't always keep me away from Google. But it was a plan of action, a list of concrete to-dos that positively impacted my health, and it set into motion my first brain-changer. In this unpredictable situation, what do I have control over? What action can I take? Sometimes it's as simple as stopping and evaluating the situation. Am I hungry? Am I tired? (Later—much, much later—when my identity as a NICU parent had faded into that of "just" a parent of three small and surprisingly loud children, I'd ask the same sort of questions. What's going on here? Are my children cranky because they are tired? Are they hungry? Am *I* cranky because I'm tired and hungry?)

For the first time in the pregnancy I had a goal and guide. Eating 4000 calories is a lot of work! That much food involves planning: shopping, preparation, execution, devouring, and cleaning up afterwards. By the time I had a snack and a nap, it was time to start over again (which cut into my Googling time). I went from mentally preparing for a horrible outcome to physically preparing for the healthiest pregnancy possible for my situation.

2
How to Build a Village

"I want to keep the news of our pregnancy to ourselves for a while," my husband Matt said. "This is a private matter and it's a scary situation. I don't want to just dump it on people."

I strongly disagreed with him. Given what the doctors had predicted, we were headed for rocky times—a month in the hospital for me and at least that much time in the hospital for our twins once they were born. This was not the time to keep news to ourselves.

People often talk about abstract concepts—patience, control, power, news—in terms of an object metaphor. We say, "I **lost** my patience." "They **grabbed** control." "He **throws** his power around." We **keep** secrets and **give** news, as if it's something tangible such as a ball just handed over to someone. ("Here—take this news. I don't want it anymore.") And negative events are often framed as having weight, as in: **unbearable** news or the **burden** of bad news. **Heavy** sorrow.

"Doctors tell us there's a 50/50 chance that the twins won't make it," Matt reminded me. "I don't want everyone to know that we're expecting and then have to give them bad news. They'd all feel terrible for us and then I'd feel responsible for unloading on them."

"We can't do this all by ourselves," I countered. "And I don't want to hide our troubles from our friends and family."

Dump.
Unload.
Give bad news.
Hide your troubles.

Metaphors are shorthand descriptions that guide how we reason. Metaphors such as ***dumping*** or ***unloading*** bad news imply that we are giving a burden to someone else. But sharing bad news is different from unloading a weight and unlike dumping a real load, ***giving*** someone bad news doesn't mean you don't have it anymore!

I wanted to physically prepare for the healthiest pregnancy possible for my situation, which meant lots of eating, lots of sleeping, lots of quality family time with my husband and two-year-old daughter.

The next step was to have a support system in place. How was my daughter going to cope with me in the hospital for a month? Who was going to make sure that my husband didn't burn the candle at both ends? We needed backup; we needed to "build a village." To me this meant staying in touch with close friends and reaching out to the people we didn't know very well, such as the parents at daycare or my husband's colleagues at work.

My husband saw it differently. While I was imagining the help we'd need if the twins or I had complications, he was imagining how selfish it seemed to dump our troubles on others. This was not an area where we could come to an agreement through compromise.

Around this same time one of my aunts was diagnosed as having terminal cancer. A spot was found on her liver. There was another one on her kidney. Matt and I watched as my mother and her four sisters shared the grim news and connected in a way I hadn't seen before—not just with my dying aunt but with each other, too. They made cross-country visits (and reportedly stayed up all night giggling). They checked in with each other weekly. One aunt quit her job so she could be near her sick sister during this time.

"Family is more important than anything else," Aunt Lulu told me.

To my mother's family sharing this sad news wasn't "unloading"; it was a rallying call that used metaphors that evoked images of power, construction, and connection.

For example:

My aunt's cancer **pulled** everyone together.

Her sisters **strengthened** their **bonds**.

They **supported** each other.

Their love had a **strong foundation**.

And of course, they **built** a village.

This is why metaphors matter. If I thought of sharing our story in terms of weights and objects, I had to agree with Matt; I didn't want to unload our burdens onto our friends, either. And when Matt talked about sharing news in terms of **pulling** together, **forming attachments**, and **building** our **support** system, the idea of telling friends didn't seem so selfish. Looking at our different metaphors rather than focusing on our different opinions helped us understand each other. It also helped us create a game plan that we were both comfortable with. And my mother's family's model support system gave us an example to follow.

It was like flipping a switch. Changing our mindset, we took action. We started a private blog to update family and friends. I connected with other parents from daycare. Matt told his boss. Suddenly we had recommendations for prenatal yoga classes, hand-me-down baby clothes from co-workers, and encouraging emails from Aunt Lulu. Best of all, when Matt and I were discouraged our network of friends was optimistic and supportive. You might say (to steal a metaphor) that our village ***lifted*** our spirits.

3
How Does Your Garden Grow?

I was so sure we were going beat the odds. Five months into our high-risk twin pregnancy and I was the picture of health. The twins were doing great. We'd found a doctors' group that specialized in high-risk pregnancies and we knew we were in good hands. Our increased effort to build our village meant lots of play dates with friends and mini-vacations to visit family. My husband and I even made time for regular Date Nights. This "positive thinking" thing was definitely paying off.

But then two weeks before the end of the second trimester and three days before Christmas, a routine ultrasound showed signs of premature labor. My doctor immediately admitted me to the hospital for mandatory bed rest and medication to help stop the contractions. One week later the contractions started again and the twins were born via emergency Cesarean section. Matt held my hand during the surgery and then he followed the boys into the Newborn Intensive Care Unit. Michael (Baby "A") weighed a pound, twelve ounces at birth. His brother Wagner (Baby "B") was born at a pound, nine ounces. They were twelve inches long.

If I had looked at the goals I had set up for myself during this risky pregnancy (carry twins to 32 weeks, avoid extensive medical intervention, have fat, healthy babies), I had failed at all of them. Of course, there's more than one way to frame failure (or success) and this is what I tried to remember as I lay in my room after surgery, waiting for Matt to come back with pictures of our babies. But really I just cycled through a list of regrets: If only I hadn't taken that yoga class. If only I hadn't flown on an airplane last month. If only, if only, if only. If only I'd done something differently then, we wouldn't be in this situation now.

For the last two years I have been raving about Carol Dweck's book *Mindset*, telling anyone who will listen how growth-mindset thinking rescued me from the "If Onlys."

On its face the growth mindset may seem that it's just about praising effort, not achievement. Dweck's book outlines habits of successful athletes, CEOs, and teachers. She looks at the components of successful family relationships. On the growth-mindset side there is cooperation, empathy, social connection, focus on effort. On the fixed-mindset side there is competition, fear, negative reinforcement, and a focus on results, regardless of how you get there.

Dweck's book is marketed in terms of "success," but it's really about how humans look at causality. Is it fixed, written in stone? Does each life event directly cause the next one—like a train of dominoes? Or is it systemic with many possibilities for nurturance and growth—such as in a positive feedback loop?

Is life like a road map? Or is it a garden?

In the fixed mindset, life is a road map. There's a **path** to success, the **road** to health. There's a right way and a wrong way, **steps** to take. Problems are bumps in the road to **get over, move past** or **leave behind you**. We look **forward** to the day when we can **look back** on this and laugh.

A growth mindset is like a garden. We **nurture, foster, protect**. Minds **blossom, grow**. We favor a healthy **environment**. Here problems are integrated into the solution. We look at the **heart** of the issue or the **root** of the problem. When we find problems, we **weed them out**.

In the same way that metaphors helped my husband and I see the other's perspective, Dweck's book helped me imagine love, education, and raising children from two different metaphoric frameworks. In each chapter she emphasizes the viewpoint that is most effective: the growth mindset. The garden.

4
Gratitude

The NICU nurses from our hospital in Berkeley knew who I was before I'd even stepped onto the floor. Not because my boys were born at just 25 weeks' gestation and were the youngest in the NICU. Not because my twins were the smallest in the NICU. The nurses in the NICU knew me because of my Aunt Rita.

"Tell your Aunt Rita thank you from us," nurses said to me, over and over as they stopped me in the hall or came by the twins' hospital room. "What a wonderful person!"

Aunt Rita (technically my husband's aunt) remembers birthdays and sends thoughtful gifts for no particular reason. She and her husband host a family reunion every summer at their home in the Midwest. *I* know that she's wonderful and fabulous but I couldn't figure out how these Berkeley nurses knew that, too.

For the first month of the twins' lives, they were in such critical condition, that each boy had a nurse standing at his bedside around the clock. The nurses showed me how to take my sons' temperature (which had to be done every four hours), change their diapers (which were smaller than an iPhone) and touch them without over-stimulating their tiny underdeveloped nervous systems (with one hand resting firmly on the top of the head and the other hand firmly on the soles of their feet—no pats, no strokes, no light brushes).

These were the kind of details I posted in our private blog for family and friends. The day the boys were born I'd recounted brief details of the birth. When Aunt Rita saw the post, she sent a huge edible bouquet to the staff at the NICU. There were stems made of carrot and celery sticks and flower blossoms carved out of pineapples.

"Thank you to the doctors and nurses who are taking care of my nephews," the card read.

"That bouquet was eaten in about twenty minutes," one of nurses told me. "Even the kale."

The metaphors for gratitude belong to a family of "moral accounting" metaphors. We say we have **debt** of gratitude or that we **pay** our thanks. We say, "I **owe** him a thank-you." Appreciation is **earned**. (Incidentally, many of the same metaphors are used for forgiveness: "I **owe** him an apology.") Moral accounting metaphors are often sub-consciously used in bribe/reward reasoning, and ideas about sacrifice, guilt, punishment, and judgment of others. Gratitude researcher Robert Emmons would have said that Rita's thank-you was *freely* given (one of the kinds of gratitude that makes us feel the happiest, for both the thank-er and those who are thanked).

The unexpected thank-you from Aunt Rita set the tone for our relationship with the doctors and nurses of the NICU (a relationship that my husband and I continue to nurture several years later). First of all, the card and thank-you gift did the obvious: it thanked the wonderful staff for their work. It was a gentle reminder to express my own gratitude regularly, frequently, and before it was *owed*. Moreover, the card's message reminded me that my boys were part of a bigger family. My boys were nephews, cousins, grandchildren, and godsons.

This is what was so enlightening to me: the card and fruit bouquet set into a motion a cascade of *freely* given thank-yous. The nurses were tickled—and touched—at this obvious display of thanks at the beginning of the boys' hospital stay. After all, it was so early. So much could still go wrong. Aunt Rita's thank you was a vote of confidence in their abilities, like a declaration of optimism. The nurses in turn thanked me profusely. Even though the bouquet didn't come from me, I still got the credit. (**Credit**—another moral accounting metaphor.)

Matt and I logged so many hours at the twins' bedside. Sometimes we just stood there, watching them. Other times we changed their diapers or rested our hands on their little bodies. We'd often sit alongside the nurses and ask questions about this medication or that oxygen setting, writing down answers that usually spawned more questions.

But because I'd walked into the NICU preceded by Aunt Rita's thank-you gift, we always had something to talk about besides preemies and grim statistical outcomes. At first our conversations with the nurses centered on edible bouquets and kale, but we also talked about weddings, favorite books, home remodels, and recipes for baked chicken. We talked about anniversary surprises for our spouses and birthday presents for favored nieces. And yes, we swapped stories about favorite aunts.

5
The Difference a Metaphor Makes

According to UC Berkeley urban legend, conceptual metaphor analysis was born from a broken heart. It was the 70s. A grad class. A young woman rushed into a linguistics seminar on metaphors. In some versions of the story, it's raining outside and the student is soaking wet.

"I'm sorry," she said. "I didn't finish my paper. I have a metaphor problem with my boyfriend."

The class stopped to discuss her metaphor problem (it was the 70s, after all. At Berkeley, no less. Of course they stopped the class to discuss her metaphor problem.)

The boyfriend had said: "We're at a dead end."

The metaphor by itself didn't need any explanation. Everyone in the room understood what it meant to tell a significant other that a relationship had reached a dead end. But what the class, including the professor, didn't understand was *how*. How did everyone know what that meant? How did they understand the intention behind the phrase? It's not in any dictionary. It's not part of a curriculum.

Week after week there was class discussion and exploration, which varies according to who is telling the story. In some versions, it's the class that catalogues and details the metaphors. In other, drier versions, it's the professor George Lakoff and his friend, visiting professor Mark Turner, who hash out the details over coffee at a café close to campus.

But regardless of the version that is fed to eager undergrads, here's what everyone agrees on: somewhere along the road, we've come to visualize life as a journey. Which is why we can understand sentences such as "somewhere along the road, we've come to visualize life as a journey."

When the boys were in the hospital, they **turned a corner** when their health improved. They were **out of the woods**, **on the road** to recovery.

When life is easy, the journey is smooth. When there are problems, they are obstacles in the road, an impediment to forward movement. In fact, the doctors would say, "We're not ready to **move forward**" or "We're **spinning our wheels**."

Life decisions are navigational ones. "We'll **cross that bridge** when we come to it." Or, "I don't want to **go too far down that road**."

Goals are destinations in the future. ***The light at the end of the tunnel.***

But here's the secret: life isn't really a journey. Progress isn't always forward movement. Or more precisely, imagining life as a journey doesn't help me when there are problems.

Here's what I can't explain to anyone except the immediate family that proofread the drafts for my thesis. If life is a journey and problems are obstacles in the road to **get over** or **move past** or **get around** or **get through**, it doesn't help me in the here and now at the NICU.

In my thesis, I examined older (often conservative) parenting books from the 70s and 80s that talked about "training" children. I compared them to the positive-discipline books that favored nurturance. The conservative parenting books used lots of journey metaphors. The goal is to keep your kids **on track**. Misbehaving is **going off the rails.** Children need **direction** and are expected to **follow** the parents' lead. Accomplishments are thought of as reaching **milestones**, as if there is one specific path and order for a developing human.

The positive discipline books, on the other hand, used garden metaphors. Children are **budding, blossoming, flowering, flourishing** when they are doing well. When they aren't, they're **withering.** There's talk of **enriching their environment**, rather than **giving them direction.**

Here's the application: if this is a journey, where we put one foot in front of the other, we are so screwed. Michael and Wagner can't breathe on their own. They can barely breathe with a machine doing it for them. I know they've had at least two blood transfusions so far. Nothing looks like progress.

But if we are in a garden, there is a lot I can do. Sun is just as nourishing as rain. Just sitting here is helpful. Help can come from unlikely suspects. In a real garden there are earthworms to enrich the soil and ladybugs to kill the aphids. Just because you don't see progress doesn't mean it's not happening. Roots dig deep into the earth and some are so strong they can split concrete. Plants have agency, too. They can take sunlight and turn it into food, which in turn becomes our oxygen. Flowers can give pleasure just by being there. It isn't a zero-sum game. It isn't a race. The cycle of growth for one seed is not the life path of another.

We're just sitting in the garden, watching the plants grow at the pace that works best for them.

My boys spent three months in the NICU. We heard many road-map metaphors. There was the **long road** to recovery. Days and weeks of **one step forward, two steps back**, when we **weren't out of the woods yet**, before we could **see the light at the end of the tunnel**.

As best I could, I transformed the road maps into gardens. The boys' incubators were greenhouses. I tried to picture blood transfusions as adding nutrients to soil. The antibiotics were the ladybugs that eat the aphids. And suddenly there was an analogy for every possibility. Surgery was like weeding or pruning. Specially-form-fitting pillows were like trellises. Love is like the sun. Sometimes it's like the rain, and you need that, too. The best part about the whole metaphor is that healthy soil and rain and sun and ladybugs and a team of gardeners work together. You might even survive the frost.

6
Empathy for the Mompetitor

In the early months of our risky twin pregnancy I sometimes felt angry, resentful, bitter or fearful. Often all I had to do was simply acknowledge these negative emotions and they would drift away. (It also helped that they were balanced by the positive emotions and actions of our friends and family.) But there was one negative emotion that I just couldn't shake—a strong dislike for a hospital mom I called "The Mompetitor."

The competitor of all competitors, the "Mompetitor" is that mother who engages you through a series of questions about your child. And then she one-ups you with the stories of her child's precocious development. If your baby said his first word at eleven months, hers spoke complete sentences at nine. If your daughter was potty-trained by three years, hers trained herself at two. If your kid performed at Lincoln Center at age twelve, her kid played Carnegie Hall at age ten.

I've met Mompetitors at the park and at the grocery store, but I didn't expect to meet one in the NICU. However, rather than brag about how her baby was bigger, better, and stronger than mine, this Mompetitor made it a point to emphasize how her baby was sicker and weaker. How many days were we in the hospital? Ninety? Her baby was in the hospital for a hundred days. How many surgeries did my babies have? One each? Hers had four. How many infections? How many blood transfusions? And so on. As if her situation were more serious than mine and therefore warranted more attention.

I found the Mompetitor to be irritating and annoying. Worst of all, I couldn't shake the notion that it was really my babies who were sicker and weaker. I was sucked into the "mompetition" and the only way I knew how to handle the situation was to walk the other way when I saw her. I could label and validate my feelings of irritation and annoyance, but it didn't make them go away. And labeling and validating the Mompetitor's feelings of superiority as insecurity just made me more irritated and annoyed.

Meanwhile, I experienced an opposite phenomenon with my family and close friends. Many had been through scary medical situations with their children, too, ranging from a toddler's tooth knocked out from a dangerous fall to a toddler's bout with cancer. Each mother was careful to emphasize her empathy toward my boys so tiny and so fragile. Sharing our stories was not a competition.

But even though we weren't trying to one-up each other, we never got out of the comparison paradigm. We still ranked our misfortunes relative to each other. My friends would end their stories with qualifiers such as "Of course, what I went through was nothing compared to what you're going through." Sometimes I would say that to them.

Subtle "life is a game" metaphors would creep into our conversations, such as **the hand we were dealt** or cases in which **the stakes were higher**. Sometimes I'd remind myself *life isn't fair*. But what I needed to remember is that life isn't a competition and to remember how life is a garden.

When my life was a competition, the Mompetitor was a rival and there was only room for one mom on the Great Martyred Mommy podium. And even though my friends and I weren't elbowing each other out of the way, we still had the pedestal. But in the garden, there are no relative rankings.

The Mompetitor didn't need me to validate her negative emotions. She wasn't scared or bitter (at least not anymore.) She was proud. And she should be! Her baby defied amazing odds. So did mine! And that's where I can empathize with her. Not (just) because I know what it's like to have a tiny newborn hooked up to a host of machines. But rather, because I know what it's like to be a mother and I know what it's like to be proud of your children. The world is a big garden. There's always room for another proud gardener.

7

Nurture Happiness and Foster Resilience

Here's the paradox that parents face: on the one hand, we want to raise our children in an environment that maximizes their potential for a joyful life. However, we can't stick our children in a bubble with the hopes that nothing bad will happen to them.

To address this issue, I had intended to write about the twins coming home after three months in the NICU and how we worried our way through the first year. We had weekly meetings with infant-development specialists and monthly medical appointments that monitored the twins' delayed development. I wanted to capture the essence of this paradox: while there are definite steps we can take to positively impact our children's happiness and resilience, our control over our children's environment is limited. I had this chapter all mapped out.

Then my husband's dad died.

Two years earlier, just before the twins were born, my father-in-law was diagnosed with a rare and stubborn form of cancer. This past Christmas we came to understand that his options for further treatment were limited. Over Easter my father-in-law entered into hospice care.

After spending spring break with the grandparents, my five-year-old daughter asked me, "Is Grandpa going to get better?"

"No," I had to tell her.

"Is Grandpa going to die?"

"Yes," I had to tell her.

Here it was, in a spontaneous conversation with my daughter, the reason we need to foster resilience. Foster Resilience. We can model a growth mindset for our children. We can practice gratitude and optimism as a family. We can have "happiness routines" that foster healthy living. But Grandpa's cancer is terminal.

"I have some books for you," the director of my daughter's preschool told me when she heard the news. She sent me home with an armful of books from the center's lending library. They had titles such as: *When Someone You Love Has Cancer: A Guide to Help Kids Cope* and *I'll Hold You and You'll Hold Me*.

"I wish I didn't have a need for such an extensive collection," she sighed.

One book in particular, *When Dinosaurs Die: A Guide to Understanding Death,* became an instant favorite with my daughter. (It's by Laura Krasny Brown and Marc Brown—you know, the guy who does the *Arthur* series.)

"Losing someone who is special to you is *very* hard to understand," the book stated simply. And: "When someone you love dies, there is no right or wrong way to feel."

Every page depicted cartoon scenes of life and death: the burial of a pet, a sick parent, a car accident, a memorial service for the Grandpa dinosaur ("Morris Saurus.") There was even a cartoon panel with two little baby dinosaur preemies hooked up to tubes and wires in little incubators.

"Just like the boys!" my daughter exclaimed, recognizing the NICU equipment even in dinosaur cartoons. We talked about how the boys were healthy now, but that they were very little and sick when they were born.

"We should give this book to Grandma," she said one night after we read it for what seemed like the fortieth time. "So she won't be so sad about Grandpa."

As I was leaving for the airport to attend the memorial, my daughter reminded me, "Did you pack the dinosaur book for Grandma?"

On the night after the funeral, friends and family came to the house to remember the man who had been uncle, brother, father, neighbor, and grandfather, among so many other roles. We cried. We laughed. We ordered pizza and watched Grandpa's favorite movie, an obscure Spaghetti Western.

The dinosaur book sat on an end table where it happened to catch the attention of some of the younger grandchildren. I watched as one by one, they nabbed the book, curled up in a corner and flipped slowly through various topics such as, "Why Does Someone Die?" "Feelings about Death," and "Ways to Remember Someone." None of the children said anything to anyone. They just silently read through the book, each child leaving it on the table where he or she had found it.

The other day, I pulled the book out again. When my daughter saw it, she wanted me to read it to her at bedtime. Afterwards, we played the game suggested on one of last pages: "I remember when..."

"I remember when Grandpa came to visit and read books to you," I began.

"I remember Grandpa's birthday party," she said.

"I remember the cards he used to make for us."

We did a few more rounds of "I remember when..." and then I kissed her and turned off the light.

I'm so sad to have lost my father-in-law. And it breaks my heart to know that my sons won't know him as we knew him—the man who was my husband's best man at our wedding, the man who sent thank-you candy to the boys' NICU nurses and read doll books to his granddaughter.

But while we are sad, we are also grateful that we have friends who recommend books to help us talk about what we're feeling. We're proud that our daughter's sadness prompted her to empathize with Grandma. We're tickled that a little thing like a book in the right place at the right time can remind us to share the happy memories of our loved ones. That's the real message: the tools we use to nurture happiness are the same ones we use to foster resilience.

8
Have Dinner as a Family

After three surgeries and two years of chemotherapy and radiation treatments, the painful decision was made for my father-in-law to enter into hospice care. For five weeks my husband and his siblings took turns flying back to their hometown where they kept vigil with their mother and took care of their father. They moved furniture and medical equipment, took notes at doctors' visits, and fielded calls from friends and neighbors.

The hospice nurse, who dropped in once a day to check on their father, clarified the dosages of morphine and described which signs to look for in the final weeks. His last piece of advice for my father-in-law was, "Make sure you eat dinner as a family. Even if you just sit there and don't eat anything. It's the most important thing you can do for morale."

A few weeks later, my father-in-law passed away.

The next day, we gathered at my husband's childhood house: his siblings, their spouses, their mother. We spent the first day cleaning, getting rid of medical supplies no longer needed, preparing the house for guests, assembling photos, drafting the eulogy, fielding telephone calls, writing thank-you notes. Sometime in the early evening a neighbor stopped by with a meal. We put down our pens and our brooms and shifted into the common space of the dinner routine, moving within the silence of a common goal.

One brother counted out the silverware we'd need. My sister-in-law folded napkins as my husband retrieved the extra chairs from the guest room. Places were set. Food was heated. It was like a well-oiled machine: eight people repeating our nightly ritual, one we had participated in as children in our respective homes, one we repeated with our own children.

We said grace; we remembered the one who was with us only in spirit. My brother-in-law recounted their father's last dinner conversation (discussing a recent *Wall Street Journal* article about dinosaur flatulence). We laughed and sighed and dabbed our eyes. The easy tone of the conversation contrasted with the weight of losing a loved one, the way you feel after a day of swimming: alert but exhausted. After dinner we cleared the table and washed the dishes, concluding the ritual.

It was calming and connecting—like meditating without even trying.

The next day the "real" rituals began: the memorial service at the funeral home, the funeral Mass at the parish, the burial at the cemetery, a lunch hosted by the church, and a final gathering for family. The list of tasks grew. There were maps to print and relatives to retrieve from the airport. There were more thank-you notes to write and more phone calls to answer. It was overwhelming and emotionally taxing. Even writing about it makes me feel drained.

But then I remember that dinner—the *ding* of the microwave, the shuffling sounds of drawers opening and closing, the light *bwap* of kitchen cabinets shutting, and the whoosh of the sliding glass door as we set the table on the patio. And as we ate: the deep sighs, the heartfelt laughter, the sniffles and tears. What a strong circle we made around that table. Not because we were trying to build morale or strengthen our family connections. Just because it was dinnertime. And that's what we do in our family. We have dinner together.

9
When the Science Falls Short

Our NICU hospital monitors every preemie graduate at a special follow-up clinic for at least two years after they've left the NICU. That's how long it takes for most preemies to "catch up" to typically developing children. When our boys were seven months old, they acted and looked like they were four months old. This adjusted age versus their chronological age was important to remember. While it isn't a big deal to have a five-month-old baby who doesn't roll over, it's quite another thing to have a nine-month-old who doesn't roll over. With so many milestones in the first two years, having an accurate idea of when our boys would hit them helped us gauge their progress.

I hated the word "milestone." It evoked the "Life as a Journey" metaphor, the idea that we're all on the same path, headed for the same destination. The doctors wanted to make sure that the twins were ***on target*** to reach their goals. Sometimes they used words such as, ***on pace*** as the twins ***charged ahead***, always evoking the journey. To be fair, they used some garden metaphors, too. We were encouraged to provide an ***enriched environment*** for our boys and ***strong***

roots. But when it came time to evaluate their progress, the milestone metaphors dominated.

When the boys were two years old, they barely had a handful of words apiece and they are were hard to understand. They were definitely not ***on target.*** It was hard not to compare their unintelligible communication with my daughter's precocious grasp of language at that age. When she was two, I recorded complicated sentences she'd quipped, such as, "So I thought to myself, why don't I read a book?" Granted, "thought" came out as "sought" and "read" sounded more like "weed." But still. My boys were talking and thinking on a much lower lever. (Which evoked another conceptual metaphor: good is up. Bad is down. An ***upright*** citizen versus a ***low*** life. Someone is ***highly*** accomplished or ***highly*** motivated. A smart student has ***high*** grades. A bad student has ***low*** ones. A ***high*** IQ versus ***low*** intelligence. Even success is measured vertically. She is moving ***up*** in the ranks. He is ***down*** on his luck.)

Extensive hearing tests with a pediatric audiologist confirmed that the boys' ears were fine. Compromised hearing was not a culprit for their language delays. There were a variety of theories and the evidence to support each one was open to interpretation. Maybe it was because they were twins. Maybe it was because they were micro preemies or because they had an older sister who did all the talking for them. One specialist suggested that we "bombard them with words." (Note the aggressive "words as weapons" metaphor.) Another instructed us only to work on language at mealtimes, forcing the boys to ask for food rather than us anticipating their needs. Still another specialist noted that the boys didn't mimic; a foundation on which language is built.

As for me, I didn't like the idea that we had a problem to *fix*, as if the boys were broken and just needed the right tools. What if this was just how they were? What if these delays were part of cognitive deficits that they were expected to have? I wanted to give them support, to meet them where they were. More importantly, my love for them wasn't tied to how many words they knew or how articulate they were as toddlers. I loved them because they were my children. I loved how they'd spend hours giggling with each other. How, if they were down for nap and one got bored, he'd try to pry open the eyelids of his sleeping brother. How they fell asleep holding hands on their first day of daycare. Their affinity for cardboard boxes.

When the boys had their final assessment at the NICU follow-up clinic, they were 29 months old. Something had switched in their brains, just as the specialists said it would. Suddenly they were sorting colored pegs the way a three-year-old would and using gerunds and pronouns the way a three-and-a-half year-old does. They had "caught up." In fact, specialists would point out that they'd scored **highly**.

"When they go to kindergarten, don't even mention it unless you want to brag," the doctor said.

And just like that, my boys weren't preemies anymore.

Truth be told, rather than feeling relief, I was steamed. They were fine. We were done. All the research and preparation—for autism, cerebral palsy, cognitive deficits. Was it for naught? I felt like I'd been studying for a test I would not have to take. And why couldn't I be grateful and move on?

This is where the science fell short. Yes, advanced technology such as EEGs confirmed that the boys' brains received signals from the ear. Early intervention specialists knew the right sort of game to teach the boys to mimic. And now all that technology could tell us that our boys were typically developing, but none of this had to do with us as a family. It had nothing to do with our love for them. Science was a tool. Cognitive linguistics highlighted areas where I could be proactive, which kept panic at bay. And, of course, cutting-edge neonatology saved their lives in the first place. But it didn't help me love them more. Similarly, uncertainty and panic didn't make me love them less.

When my daughter was born and I held her in my arms, I didn't have to question if I loved her. It was a different kind of love—it wasn't the familial love I was used to. Or the habitual affection. Or the blinding passion of a crush. It was different. I felt connected to her. Not metaphorically. Physically. I could feel it in my bones and my organs and of course, in the tingling of my breasts a physical attachment. Which, just a few hours earlier had been exactly that. I didn't have to consciously think about how to love her. It was just there. (That's not to say that I *liked* her. She was really loud. A baby soprano.)

Somehow even the fact that she was loud and annoying meant that I didn't have to question whether or not I loved her. I felt her. We bonded. It was love.

The boys were different. Partly because I couldn't hold them. Partly because we were always waiting for the other shoe to drop. We braced for quick, swift bad news such as a phone call that might tell us tragedy struck during the night, that while we were home in our beds, the boys were sleeping in their isolettes, struggling for breath. Or that maybe the news would be gradual but just as devastating.

In the first days after they were born, I would stand paralyzed in front of the boys' isolettes. I couldn't make their lungs stronger. I couldn't make their hearts beat regularly. I couldn't comfort them. I felt I would treasure my time with them differently if I knew for certain they wouldn't make it. I was afraid to think of them as "my sons."

They went a week without names. My husband and I weren't sure if we would have to fill out death certificates as well as birth certificates. Without saying it aloud, we both knew that we'd give our sons one set of family names if they survived and different names in memoriam.

Their eyes were puffy. The sides of their heads were flat. The skin on their cheeks puckered and pulled from the tape that secured various tubes for breathing and feeding. It would be months before they looked like fresh, healthy newborns.

But the nurses always thought of my twins as tiny people with personalities and preferences—regardless of what they looked like or what the odds against them were.

"Michael loves his bath," they'd tell me. "He always opens his eyes."

Or—"Wagner knows your voice. See? Look at his oxygen-saturation numbers."

From the nurses I found out that Michael preferred to

sleep on his tummy and hated to have his diaper changed. That Wagner would sleep through both his bath and his diaper change and that he loved to get a few drops of breast milk on his tongue.

The nurses made scrapbook pages that boasted of the twins' milestones ("I'm 28 weeks!") and hung them around the boys' room. They took photographs of moments I would have never seen otherwise: Michael and Wagner in an open crib, cheeks pressed against each other. Michael and Wagner nose-to-nose and clasping hands.

I watched the nurses coo and fuss over the twins. At the same time, they also were delivering life-saving care. It gave me permission to love my boys just the way they were.

It's great that Matt and I could unfold our panic with neat, tidy metaphors. Discovering that the organs of the body work together in a systemic nature, remembering that worst-case scenarios are salient exemplars were like a trail of bread crumbs that led to a calm place of mind and spirit. They helped us get through the NICU one day at a time. But cognitive science did not model love. That came from the loving experts who took care of our babies.

Love is not a thing that you dish out like ice cream or pudding. Love is not an investment—the notion that what you give now correlates to what you'll get back later.

Love is like sunshine. The heat of summer may be different from gentle spring sunlight, but it's still the sun. It may look different in the morning than it does at noon, but it's still sun. And on cloudy days when it doesn't look like it's there at all, it still gives light.

SUPPLEMENTAL READING

Here's a partial list of books that were invaluable to me. They helped me write a thesis. More importantly, they helped me through a very difficult time.

George Lakoff
Metaphors We Live By

I was a freshman in college when I first read George Lakoff (another way to say that is that I was 35 years old when I came across Lakoff.) Light bulbs went on in my head. It was an academic article that merely pointed out the presence of metaphor in language. The concept of an idea as an object—we *give* ideas; we *take* ideas; we *steal* ideas; some ideas are half-baked, etc.—was somehow both new to me and known to me at the same time. I'd never stopped to think how knowledge could be conceptualized as seeing and yet once I read the idea I could come up with a dozen metaphors on my own to prove the point.

He's not too **bright**.
I was **in the dark** *the whole meeting.*
Enlighten *me.*
See *what I mean?*

Since *Metaphors We Live By* was published in 1980, George Lakoff has continued to examine the metaphors we unconsciously use to communicate. For the past two decades he has focused on the metaphors used in politics as a way to describe progressive and conservative messaging. Subsequent books are *Don't Think of an Elephant, Moral Politics, Thinking Points,* and *The Political Mind*, among others. Of all of his books and textbooks, *Don't Think of an Elephant* is probably the easiest to read and get the gist of his work. *Metaphors We Live By* is an academic text, in other words, it's not much of a beach read. But it also doesn't take a lot to skim through the chapters and see how multi- dimensional language is.

Carol S. Dweck
Mindset: The New Psychology of Success

Carol S. Dweck's *Mindset: The New Psychology of Success* is no longer new. Her ideas of a growth mindset versus a fixed mindset are now a staple for many educators looking for ways to motivate children without bribing them. Dweck is a professor and researcher at Stanford. Her book is backed by solid research and unlike Lakoff's academically worded works, *Mindset* is accessible to a larger audience who doesn't want to wade through a thick text of "prof-speak." Available on Amazon but do your community a favor and order it through your neighborhood bookstore.

Christine Carter
Raising Happiness: 10 Simple Steps for More Joyful Kids and Happier Parents

Christine Carter has moved on from her position as executive director of the Greater Good Science Center and offers parenting classes through her website, christinecarter.com. She's the author of two books: *Raising Happiness: 10 Simple Steps for More Joyful Kids and Happier Parents* and *The Sweet Spot*. *Raising Happiness* is the book that is referred to in this text, as it directly relates to parenting.

Laura Krasny Brown and Marc Brown
When Dinosaurs Die: A Guide to Understanding Death

This age-appropriate book covers everything from death of an older family member to suicide, accidental death, drug overdose, and preemie babies. It acknowledges social and religious customs associated with death and afterlife. This is not the sort of book that you pick up and read to your kid because you're not sure how to talk about death and you want a book to do it for you. You'll want to explain as you go along. This is a conversation-starter and it opens the door for discussion. I appreciated the simple talk—"No one knows for sure what happens when we die, but some people believe X."

I liked that it wasn't preachy and that it's not a silver-linings sort of book. We're sad when someone dies, especially when it's someone we love. We don't always have answers and there are many ways to honor their memory. On Amazon, this book is listed as suggested reading for ages 4–7. I'd say this is an all-ages book. At my father-in-law's memorial, the book lay on a coffee table where it caught the eye of several of my nieces and nephews in the eight-to-tween range.

Alison Gopnik, all of it

As researcher and director of Gopnik Cognitive Development Lab at UC Berkeley, Alison Gopnik focuses on how young children learn about their environment. Her books are *The Scientist in the Crib*, *The Philosophical Baby*, and *The Gardener and the Carpenter*. If you want to know what's going on in your kid's head as she learns about her environment, start with *The Scientist in the Crib* and work your way to most her most recent. I love Gopnik's work. It's scientifically based and while it's accessible to those of us who don't spend our days reading academic papers, it's not dumbed down.

The Greater Good Science Center

The Greater Good Science Center, a UC Berkeley center, is part of the university's Institute of Human Development. It's a research center as well as a collection of online resources. Their workshops, seminars, and website articles focus on positive psychology and the scientific research behind gratitude, altruism, and empathy. See for yourself: http://greatergood.berkeley.edu/

Janine Kovac

"A Cognitive Linguistic Analysis of Parenting"

Yes, I did. I just referenced my own work as supplemental reading. It's my undergrad thesis. I'll be honest. It's clearly the work of someone who is almost out of college and is trying to impress by writing really long sentences. But some of those sentences are still pretty informative and if nothing else, might inspire you to Google something even more informative on moral accounting, gratitude research, or positive parenting. Think of it as a gateway book for cognitive science. You can find it at my website: janinekovac.com.

ACKNOWLEDGEMENTS

Dad, thank you for turning me on to the subtleties of language and metaphor long before I'd ever heard of this thing called "cognitive science."

Mom, thank you for all the behind-the-scenes support before, during, and after our cozy family of three exploded into a brood of five. You are my role model, the kind of mother I want to be for my family.

George Lakoff, thank you for your patience, for being an advisor as I trudged my way through my thesis. You continue to inspire me with your insight.

Christine Carter, I know it looked like stalking; it was really just a walk of admiration. Thank you for the opportunity to post some of this material on your Raising Happiness blog. Thank you for your support and guidance.

Alison Gopnik, I loved your course. I loved your books. But what speaks loudest to me is breath you've given to parenting as a science complete with hypotheses, data, and conclusions.

Rachel, thank you for keeping me honest. Mary, Joanne, and Alexandra, thank you for cheering me on. Lorrie, thank you for the eagle eyes.

To Alison Brooks and the Alta Bates NICU, thank you for teaching our family to breathe in more ways than one. Thank you for your tireless work on behalf of preemies and your support of families. We are a happier and healthier family as a direct result of your work and outreach.

Marian, Jackie, Jason, and Elroy. Thank you for being my village.

Aunt Rita and the Kovacs. CoR4Evah. Fist bump. Word.

Matt! I probably should have admitted that you cooked all those meals when I was pregnant. Thank you for feeding me. Thank you for proofreading. Thank you in advance for all the feeding and proofreading still to come.

Kids—I love you. Go to bed.

ABOUT THE AUTHOR

Janine Kovac was a professional ballet dancer and a software engineer before studying cognitive science at UC Berkeley She graduated *magna cum laude* one month shy of her 40th birthday, receiving the 2009 Glushko Prize for distinguished undergraduate research in cognitive science for her thesis, "A Cognitive Linguistic Analysis of Parenting."

She thought she was on track to go to graduate school but a surprise twin pregnancy changed all that.

Today Janine works for Litquake, San Francisco's literary festival as web maven and event producer. She's a founding member of the 501(c)3 nonprofit writing group Write on Mamas and co-founder of the consulting firm Moxie Road Productions. From 2015 to 2017, she directed the San Francisco production of Listen To Your Mother, a nationwide reading series in celebration of Mother's Day.

Her writing has appeared on Salon.com, RaisingHappiness.com, and in *Pregnancy and Newborn* magazine. She's been anthologized in *Mamas Write: 29 Tales of Truth, Wit, and Grit*, *Multiples Illuminated* and *Nothing But the Truth, So Help Me God*. Her memoir *Spinning: Choreography for Coming Home* was a 2017 semi-finalist for Publishers

Weekly's BookLife prize.

When she's not making lunches and volunteering in her children's classroom (okay, the husband makes the lunches), Janine is writing. She is a three-time scholarship recipient (and four-time participant) of the Squaw Valley Community of Writers. She's a former resident of Hedgebrook and the Mineral School. In 2016 she received an Elizabeth George Foundation Fellowship.

Janine is still an active member of the NICU community and is a regular contributor to a regional newsletter for parents of preemies. In her spare time, Janine teaches ballet to third-graders. She lives in Oakland, California with her husband and their three children.

Visit her at janinekovac.com.

A SNEAK PEEK OF

Spinning

CHOREOGRAPHY for COMING HOME

A MOTHER'S MEMOIR

2017 semifinalist for
Publishers Weekly's BookLife Prize

Prologue

The one skill that can still be honed in a dancer's aging body is her memory. More than once I got a role simply because I was the only dancer who knew what to remember and what to push aside.

When you start to learn choreography, your mind is blank. It's at its freshest for remembering steps. This is not a good thing because choreographers change their minds. They invent combinations of turns, leaps, and lifts and often can't remember what they've done. They rely on the dancers to record and demonstrate.

Turn on the count of four.

No, wait—make it two turns.

What happens if you jump first and then turn?

Lift the left leg instead of the right.

Go back to the third version.

Not that version. The one before.

Every pattern is a sequence of absolute truth. When you dance, the choreography has to look like the only version that has ever existed. The other versions lie dormant in your muscles' memory, just in case.

Dress Rhearsal

I am dozing in my bed in the hospital when I feel the pains—a gas bubble that won't go up or down. It just stays there and pulses. Maybe it's the enchiladas that I ate for lunch. Maybe it is just gas. Unfortunately, it feels sharper, closer to labor pains.

It's the day before New Year's Eve, 2009. My twins aren't due until Easter. April 10th, to be exact. Not now. Not at only twenty-five weeks and four days' gestation.

My room is bright and cheery—even when it's rainy outside, like today. There's a huge flower arrangement on the windowsill, a present from my in-laws. In the corner is a tiny plastic Christmas tree from Walgreens. Its fiber-optic branches glow from yellow to green to blue to purple. They are decorated with scraps of my daughter Chiara's preschool art, fastened to the plastic needles with paper clips my husband brought from work.

I look to my bedside table for the book my stepmom gave me about twin pregnancies. It's not there anymore. She must have given it to my nurse already. There's another woman here who has the same kind of risky pregnancy and today in the support group I told her she could have one of my books. If the book were still here, I might look up the chapter on labor. But then again, I'm in the antepartum unit, just down the hall from the labor and delivery ward. If I need expert advice, all I have to do is call the nurse.

Maybe this is a false alarm, more Braxton-Hicks contractions such as the ones I had last night. My husband Matt was fast asleep in the pullout chair. For a week now, he'd been putting Chiara to sleep in her bed at home just two miles away and leaving her in the care of a relative so he could stay with me. Last week it had been my brother. This week it was my sister Jackie and stepmom Marian. Next week, it would be my mother. Matt was always careful to return home just before dawn to be with Chiara when she awoke, none the wiser.

I put my hands on my belly. It was so different from being pregnant with one child. I could feel two different energies, two different personalities almost. The nurses didn't believe me when I told them that I could tell the twins apart from how they moved inside me, but Matt did. One baby moved in flutters and zips. I called him the Red Baby. The other one seemed to mosey along, grooving to an imaginary reggae beat. I called him the Blue Baby. I could never explain why I saw those colors and not purple or green or orange, outside of the technical term for it: synesthesia. I saw colors when I read words, heard music, or felt my babies move. The Red Baby simply felt red while the Blue Baby felt blue. Just like Mozart's music was pastel pink and Prokofiev was midnight blue. Just like Chiara was a bright sunny yellow.

Usually just the warmth of my palms on my skin was

enough to get the twins to dance. But this time, instead of red and blue undulations, I feel the black-and-gray streaks of a muscle spasm. A cramp. A contraction?

That's what makes this afternoon's discomfort so different from last night's. That pain felt nebulous and scattered; this feels focused, determined. Rhythmic. Pressure that momentarily interrupts my breath.

I'm not supposed to get out of bed, but if it is gas, moving around could help. I walk the few steps to my bathroom. But instead of the slow, lumbering movements I've been making of late, I'm quick, light, the way you dance on a broken foot to keep from feeling the pain.

There is a squeezing. A pull. Not the outward push of air against abdomen but abdomen against womb. No, no, no, please don't be that kind of squeezing. Not now. Not yet. Ten weeks from now, fine. Eight weeks from now—even three weeks from now. But not now.

I feel woozy, like I might slip. I hold onto the metal rail for balance and the edges of my vision go gray and fuzzy. But the center of my sight—the wastebasket, the tile floor, the edge of the sink—is all crystal clear, even though I'm not wearing my glasses. I pull on the cord labeled "Call Nurse."

Leaning against the bathroom door, I'm trying to breathe and at the same time I'm trying not to breathe. I watch myself from above—a woman with dark hair in a light green hospital gown and an enormous belly stretched taut. I can't see my face; I can only see my back. There's a tug—as if gravity is pulling me to the ground, reaching inside, and sucking life out.

JANINE KOVAC

Everyone thinks that an out-of-body experience means watching yourself from the rafters. That's just the visual perspective. There's also the feeling of being deeply rooted inside your vital organs, as if your heart were the center of the universe. In the same breath you observe from the outside and feel from within.

The first time I felt this was during a dress rehearsal in Germany in a ballet that was set to one of Bach's flute concertos. From the catwalks up above I watched myself dance. On the stage below I felt my arms lift and my feet point. A flurry of white chiffon in white satin pointe shoes. I was so startled I nearly tripped and took my partner down with me. But in the split second between falling and soaring I realized I could choose to stay in this in-between land of actively moving my limbs and passively watching them. I balanced in the contradiction of the moment. It felt like flying.

When a scratchy voice comes through on the intercom I say, "I think I'm in labor."

Spinning: Choreography for Coming Home **is available online or from your favorite independent bookstore.**

www.ingramcontent.com/pod-product-compliance
Lightning Source LLC
Chambersburg PA
CBHW031429290426
44110CB00011B/586